Emotio Intelligence Excellence

The Essential "What, Why and How" To Unlocking Life's Potential

By Colette Lees

www.emotionalintelligence-training.com

General Information

About the Author

Colette Lees is a sought-after trainer and speaker on Emotional Intelligence and is founder of Xcellence International, delivering courses worldwide.

Colette has been involved in personal and professional development for more than 20 years. She has an MBA and has been a Senior Lecturer for several years at a one of the North of England's leading Business Universities.

Prior to her academic career, Colette ran several retail businesses of her own and was a senior manager with a number of international companies. Today she holds directorships with several private companies in the UK and USA where she acts as a consultant, advisor and coach.

Colette describes herself as a 'practitioner' of her subject. Her hands-on approach and depth of understanding of business structures, real world situations and relationships provide a unique insight and allow interventions which go beyond the limits of traditional delivery.

She has a challenging coaching style and her trainings are designed to be thought-provoking while dramatically shifting behaviours. Her aim is to teach Emotional Intelligence in a way that is both accessible and effective.

Colette's passion for people and their personal and professional development is the driving force behind her career and her interest in spreading the word about the power of Emotional Intelligence.

Contents

Introduction

Everything we achieve in life depends on two vital relationships – the relationship we have with ourselves and the relationship we have with others around us.

Emotional Intelligence is the key to understanding, explaining and improving these relationships.

This enables us to achieve greater success as individuals and in the important groups we are part of such as families, businesses and other organisations.

When I first came across the concept of Emotional Intelligence, I immediately felt I'd found a "missing link".

This was something that brought together several of the concepts I'd previously learned in many years working in large corporations, running my own business and teaching in an academic environment.

All of a sudden, I found I had a language to explain things that I felt I'd known instinctively for years.

Over time, I've introduced the concept in teaching and in my work as a coach and I've discovered that many others have seen great benefits from learning about Emotional Intelligence.

The concept is becoming more widely recognised and our ability to learn, measure and improve how we work with our emotions is improving all the time.

The range of people and organisations recognising Emotional Intelligence as a valuable tool in personal and organisation growth includes governments, global corporations, leading executives and many entrepreneurs.

Filling the Gap

The big challenge of Emotional Intelligence is that many people have heard of it but few can define what it is. Even fewer know how to use or develop it.

On the one hand, there are many academic textbooks which go into great detail. On the other, there are some more popular texts that cover Emotional Intelligence but often lack the necessary depth to be truly valuable.

So, drawing on my academic experience, I set out to create a guide to Emotional Intelligence that builds accurately on the detailed research on the topic.

At the same time, from my day-to-day experience of working with organisations and individual coaching clients, I saw the need for a more practical guide that helps people actually make use of the information.

- So this book is designed in the following stages:
- Introduces you to the concept of Emotional Intelligence.
- Identifies its key elements.
- Shows how these elements relate to each other.
- Demonstrates how to incorporate Emotional Intelligence in your personal and professional life.

In the process of doing that, you will have the opportunity to:

- Discover how emotions affect your daily decisions and actions.
- Experiment with new behaviours.
- Identify how learning about Emotional Intelligence can benefit you.
- Expand your emotional vocabulary to increase your choices.
- Identify patterns of thoughts and behaviours that limit your Emotional Intelligence and discover how to change them.

I hope this book motivates you to learn more about Emotional Intelligence and that it will help you in all areas of your life.

1. Discovering the Power of Emotional Intelligence

Emotional Intelligence provides a whole new dimension to the way we view ourselves and our relationships with others.

This helps us achieve better outcomes in our work and personal lives.

Almost everyone who discovers Emotional Intelligence has already spent a good deal of time learning traditional approaches to management and personal development such as Belbin, Myers-Briggs, NLP and similar concepts.

Emotional Intelligence is not about replacing any of these.

These – and many others – are valuable resources to have in your toolbox for getting better results for yourself and in business.

However, Emotional Intelligence is something quite different.

It acts more like a guide book you can use to help you get the best out of all the other tools you have at your disposal.

It provides a clear framework and common language that enables you to bring other elements together and get better results.

The key is that it rests on accepting that emotions play an important role in delivering the success we desire as organisations and individuals.

The Importance of Emotions

We are often encouraged to believe that we should put emotions aside and not give in to our feelings.

However, the truth is that our emotions can override our thought processes and our ability to make changes in our lives.

- When you go into a meeting and you are angry about something that happened beforehand, it inevitably affects the way that meeting will go.
- If a change is needed in the way you work, your ability to make that change successfully will be influenced by the degree of confidence you have in making the change.
- If you are the leader of a team, the way you think and act will have a big influence on the other members of the team.
- Your personal relationships will be shaped by the previous experiences you – and the others involved – bring to these relationships.
- The pleasure you get out of your free time will depend on how well you handle issues that arise in your working life.

If we ignore emotions – or don't have a way to take them into account – we lose a crucial part of the jigsaw.

The reality is that our emotions influence our thought processes and our decisions.

So when we know how to recognise and manage those emotions – and take into account the emotions of others – we can get better results.

Being able to do this enables us to quickly and correctly identify what needs to happen in any situation and then take action to make sure it does happen.

> *Our emotions influence our thought processes and our decisions.*

The Traditional Approach

The traditional approach to making such changes is to focus on skills and tasks and to leave emotions aside.

For example, training often gives us the "What" of management theory and personal development.

It answers questions such as:

- What is stress?
- What is conflict?

- What is assertiveness?
- What is your leadership style?

However, that is only part of the equation as emotions clearly influence the outcome in all of these situations.

The power of Emotional Intelligence is that it goes beyond the "What" to help you build on your existing learning, personal development and leadership knowledge.

It shows you "How To" use what you already know to tackle situations so that you get the best results possible in all circumstances.

Often it provides the key to unlock what we have previously learned but may have been unable to fully implement.

It shows us how to make the changes necessary for a happier, more fulfilling life.

Managing Our Emotions

Although Emotional Intelligence is not a new concept, the ability to use it effectively to help organisations and individuals become more successful is relatively new – and indeed is still evolving.

Using what we know about emotions to develop the right personal competencies is important in making a difference in our lives and in our relationships.

Although the basis of our emotions – our emotional memory – is formed early in our lives, more attention is now being paid to emotional adult development.

> *Emotional Intelligence shows us how to make the changes necessary for a happier, more fulfilling life.*

At the same time, awareness of the power of emotional communication is growing. We are learning more about:

- The language needed to explain Emotional Intelligence.
- The means by which to develop it.
- The hazards of ignoring the importance of emotional health.

Developing Emotional Literacy

For many of us, the communication of Emotional Intelligence requires a whole new language – known as Emotional Literacy.

There is substantial evidence that traditional measures of intelligence on their own are not adequate predictors of success. Emotional Intelligence helps integrate the intellectual and emotional aspects – aiding development of both.

It builds on our existing strengths to establish a platform of competencies which can be taught and developed with any individual.

It is this positive approach that makes the difference when building relationships with others and ourselves.

Building Blocks

Emotional Intelligence really provides a more complete framework for our development as people – whether it's in our work, in our personal relationships or any other area of our lives.

It is a powerful tool especially working alongside coaching – whether on a business or personal level. The key is that it really gets to the heart of what is going on within an individual at any time – and gives them internal clarity as well as a language to be able to share it with others.

It provides building blocks that help us break down what is happening and then find a way to rebuild it more effectively. That's why it is fast becoming recognised as a key ingredient in personal and professional development.

Supported by academic theory and world-class business practice, Emotional Intelligence is providing an increasingly powerful foundation for sustained development.

Using Emotional Intelligence

However Emotional Intelligence is not just theory. Here are some ways it can be used in a practical way:

- **Recruitment:** Choosing the right people; finding the right job.
- **Retention:** Keeping the best people; staying in the right job.
- **Team building:** Getting the best out of groups you lead or are part of.
- **Succession Planning:** Keeping the right people; planning your career.
- **Leadership Development:** Developing your skills or your best people.
- **Stress management:** Helping you and others perform at your best.
- **Relationship issues**: Getting on better with others at work or at home.
- **Working with children:** Becoming a better parent or teacher.
- **Executive development:** Enhancing key skills in top people.

In fact, there is plenty evidence that there is not a single area of life that is not affected by Emotional Intelligence.

As we go through the book, we'll cover examples from some of these situations and many more to see how it works in practice.

> *Emotional Intelligence is fast becoming recognised as a key ingredient in personal and professional development.*

2. Understanding Emotional Intelligence

It has long been recognised that traditional measures of intelligence and technical skill are inadequate on their own as predictors of success.

The challenge has been finding a way of measuring the other key elements.

You can trace references to Emotional Intelligence and its implications for success and personal fulfilment as far back as Socrates and Aristotle.

For example, Aristotle said:

> *"Anyone can become angry…that is easy. But to be angry with the right person, to the right degree, at the right time, for the right purpose, and in the right way…that is not easy."*

As we'll see, that really gets to the root of what Emotional Intelligence is about.

Charles Darwin suggested that survival – whether in animal or human development – was not a question of being the fittest. It was about being the most able to adapt to change.

In the human environment, there is constant change and we depend on the others around us. That means social skills were needed for humans to survive and prosper.

Development of Emotional Intelligence

Early in the twentieth century, research by Elton Mayo and Robert Thorndike into social intelligence suggested that scientific measures

Scientific measures alone could not predict the success of teams or individuals.

alone could not predict the success of teams or individuals and they argued that social and emotional factors were additional influencers.

Then David McClelland's research at Harvard Business School into Emotional Intelligence reported a need to move beyond traditional measures, which he termed "threshold competencies" towards something more useful in the form of "distinguishing competencies".

These are all identified under the larger concept of Emotional Intelligence.

In contrast to the common thinking of the time, McClelland suggested that:

> *"To hire or promote the best person for the job… [you should] discard the standard criteria of IQ, technical skills and personality… and first study… those… who were outstanding performers in their job".*

This was endorsed by Howard Gardner's research on multiple intelligences.

Gardner recognised that:

- *Intelligence is far more than just problem-solving, far more than the degree classification or level of academic achievement.*
- *Individuals have strengths in different areas of behaviour – there are different ways of "being smart".*

He also suggested that IQ should not be seen as the only predictor of success.

He defined seven measures of intelligence:

- Social
- Musical
- Spatial
- Intellect
- Linguistic
- Intrapersonal
- Interpersonal

Intrapersonal and Interpersonal in particular are competencies found in most Emotional Intelligence models.

In 1990, two American university professors, John Mayer and Peter Salovey, published work trying to develop a way of measuring the difference between peoples' abilities in the area of emotions.

They found that some people were better than others at:

- Identifying their own feelings.
- Identifying the feelings of others.
- Solving problems involving emotional issues.

They titled one paper "Emotional Intelligence", which they defined as follows:

"A form of social intelligence that involves the ability to monitor one's own and others' feelings and emotions, to discriminate among them, and to use this information to guide one's thinking and action."

More recently, science has been backing up many of these conclusions through studies of MRI scans which demonstrate what is actually going on inside the brain when various emotions are being played out.

They are putting people into situations where certain emotions are being stimulated and looking at the responses of the brain to show how it affects cognitive ability and decision-making processes.

For example one UCLA study showed that naming emotions created a very specific type of brain activity that actually reduced emotional reactions.

> *Thoughts and feelings working together produce a more desirable outcome.*

The implication was that getting your thoughts and feelings working together produced a more desirable outcome than trying to ignore the feelings.

The Goleman Effect

Despite the long history of the development of Emotional Intelligence, it is Daniel Goleman who is credited with the popularisation of the term – in particular in the business arena.

In 1995, his book "Emotional Intelligence" – which drew together research on the brain, emotions, and behaviour – became an international best seller.

The book made it to the cover of Time Magazine and the New York Times bestseller list. Meanwhile, Goleman appeared on American television shows such as Oprah and Dr. Phil.

In 1998, his second book "Working with Emotional Intelligence" widened the definition of Emotional Intelligence stating it consisted of 25 "skills, abilities and competencies".

Since then there has been an impressive and growing body of research suggesting that the abilities associated with Emotional Intelligence are important for success in many areas of life.

Today a Google search for Emotional Intelligence yields over 20 million results.

Emotional Intelligence in Business

Last century, Fredrick Taylor was one of the driving forces behind the success of Ford's car production. Henry Ford was seen as the expert on selling cars and he used Taylor's scientific methods to achieve the best way of producing them.

One of the ways Taylor helped develop the production line was that he put groups of people together and looked at why some teams outperformed others.

Taylor discovered that success wasn't only to do with their level of intellectual ability or technical skill.

While his work involved elements of maximising efficiency – the famous "time and motion" studies – he also noticed that success depended heavily on their feelings of affiliation, of being involved, and being supported by the team members that they were with.

This sparked some of the academic and scientific research into what you could say philosophers have always known. The scientists are now catching up.

Although it was not research specifically into Emotional Intelligence, there was some very interesting work carried out by John Kay, who went on to become a professor at Cambridge University.

He was commissioned to do some work and he wrote a book based on it called "The Foundations of Corporate Success."

He looked at a wide range of companies to find out why some are more successful than others. He wanted to know why some companies remain successful in the long-term – in business terminology they have a "sustainable competitive advantage".

What he found was that there were three distinguishing factors that gave them this sustainable competitive advantage.

- The first one was innovation.
- The next was reputation.
- The third one he termed as "architecture".

Architecture to him was about the internal and external relationships that the companies had e.g. with their employees or suppliers which were built up over a long period of time.

The ability to build trust, loyalty and integrity may seem like a "soft skill" but he was saying it was one of the defining characteristics of companies who had been successful over a long period.

Kay said if you could build architecture and combine that with reputation or innovation, then you've really got something.

Kay's book was published in 1995 – the same year Daniel Goleman published "Emotional Intelligence".

In there, when Goleman defined Emotional Intelligence, he used the same terminology. He also talked about "architecture".

Entirely different research coming together on the other side of the world at the same time was saying exactly the same thing.

Goleman looked at research in social areas, in business and in education and he identified an "architecture of relationships".

This architecture was about how people form relationships and how that could then be broken down to identify what's going on so it could be rebuilt and shown to others.

> *Trust, loyalty and integrity may seem "soft skills" but they are defining characteristics of successful companies.*

His definition of Emotional Intelligence was saying something very similar in the personal and professional world as John Kay was identifying in business research on the other side of the world at the time.

The Emotional Intelligence Revolution

The emotional intelligence revolution has already impacted the education and corporate worlds.

There is a growing recognition that when you put together measures of intellect and measures of emotion, you have a very strong platform for predicting success.

There are several different approaches and models of Emotional Intelligence but the Goleman approach is the most-widely used. This is how Goleman defines Emotional Intelligence.

> *"The capacity for recognising our own feelings – and those of others – for motivating ourselves, for managing emotions well in ourselves and in our relationships."*

The Goleman model of Emotional Intelligence is based on the following four factors or quadrants:

- Self-Awareness
- Self-Management
- Social Awareness
- Relationship Management

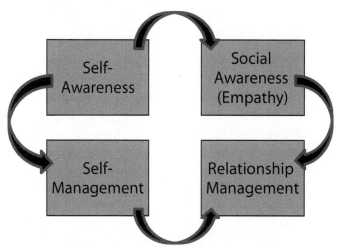

When you start to break the concept down in this way, it enables you to tackle each of the elements individually.

We then break the concept down further by splitting each quadrant into more specific criteria or Emotional Competencies.

Goleman's model features 21 different Emotional Competencies spread across the four quadrants.

No-one is going to excel in all four quadrants or all 21 competencies at one time.

The most successful people have high ratings in several of the competencies.

Your skills will already be more developed in some than in others so the key is to decide which priorities to focus on based on where you are right now.

- Self-Awareness is where we tackle the source of the issue not the symptom. This is the key to the foundation of maintained change.
- Self-Management is where we take action.
- Social Awareness is where we identify how best to work effectively with others.
- Relationship Management is how we work with others using techniques such as conflict management, influence, negotiation and team building.

In the following chapters, we will go through each of these elements individually.

Few people score highly in all but what we find is that the most successful people have high ratings in more than one element.

That's why being able to improve your ratings in different areas can make a big difference to the success you achieve in all areas of your life.

Emotional Intelligence really is that powerful!

3. Developing Self Awareness

The first element of Emotional Intelligence is Self-Awareness and it is the foundation on which the other elements are built.

Without Self-Awareness it is extremely difficult, perhaps even impossible, to develop ourselves in the areas of Self-Management, Social Awareness and Relationship Management.

That's why I believe Self-Awareness is the most important of the four quadrants.

The reality is that if you don't recognise that something needs to be done, it's going to be very hard for you to do anything about it.

We define Self–Awareness as follows:

> *"A realistic assessment of our own abilities; knowing our internal states, preferences, resources and intuitions. Awareness of moods and thoughts about that mood and using those preferences to guide our decision-making."*

In common with the other areas of Emotional Intelligence, Self-Awareness is sub-divided into separate competencies. These are as follows:

- **Emotional Self-Awareness:** Ability to read our own emotions and recognise their impact.
- **Accurate Self-Assessment:** Ability to correctly measure our own strengths and weakness.
- **Self-Confidence:** Appreciation of our own worth and belief that we can build on our strengths.

[More detailed descriptions are in the glossary at the back.]

Clearly some people may score very well in one or two of the individual competencies and not so well in others. Being able to break them up in this way gives us something more specific to work on.

Although Self-Awareness has only three competencies – while some of the other quadrants have several – Self-Awareness is still, I believe, the most important quadrant.

Just Common Sense

It can often be tempting to view a lot of Emotional Intelligence as simply being obvious and common sense.

However, the truth is that people don't always act on things they believe to be common sense.

A key strength of Emotional Intelligence is that it helps bring to the surface things we already know intuitively so that we can act on the information.

For example, while we may feel we are self-aware:

- We may be aware of our own emotions but don't realise their real impact on ourselves or on others.
- We may feel we have a clear picture of our own strengths and abilities but it may not be shared by others. This could be leading us in the wrong direction or holding us back.
- We may not have a true picture of the value we bring to a situation and therefore limit our potential to make an impact.

On that basis, the more we can learn about ways to get a true Self-Assessment, the greater contribution we can make.

As we work through this book, we'll be using a series of brief exercises to help build your understanding of Emotional Intelligence and help you use it to get better results. The first exercise is about understanding Self-Awareness better.

Exercise 1: How You Will Be Remembered

Imagine you have the opportunity to write your own obituary – based on your life until now. Think about this the way you would like it to be written – how you would like to be remembered – and take a few minutes to write out what you would want to appear in that obituary.

Learning About Yourself

So, what did you discover about yourself when writing your own obituary? Does it focus on what you have done or on what kind of person you are?

Does it present you the way you want to be remembered – e.g. as a loving parent, trusted friend or loyal employee?

It's interesting to reflect on others you remember and consider whether you think of them based on who they were or what they have achieved.

We are taught to focus on our goals – what we can achieve – and there is a place for that in our lives. However, we need to think about our values too – who we are and what is important to us.

If we only define ourselves by what we do and what we have achieved we miss out on the richness of the personal qualities which make up the very essence of who we are. So as you look over your obituary…

> *A Johnson & Johnson survey demonstrated a strong link between emotional competence and superior performance in leaders.*

- What disconnects have you identified between who you want to be remembered as and how you are living now?
- Are there values you have stopped living by, personal competencies you would like to develop or qualities you have neglected?

The fact is, if we define ourselves only by what we have achieved, we are limiting our self-awareness. This limits our lives in so many ways.

This exercise allows us to value areas we may have previously overlooked or to take what we are instinctively good at and make it explicit. You should also bear in mind that if you are limiting the way you define yourself, you may also be limiting the way you define others.

This exercise is a good start on your journey to self-awareness. Let's continue that journey with another exercise.

Exercise 2: Platform for Strengths

This exercise is in two parts.

In the first part, think of something you are good at and think about how you came to be good at it. You can choose anything you are good at whether it is related to work, hobbies or your personal life.

Now, think about how you know you are good at what you have chosen.

Have a look now at the reasons you know you are good at what you chose.

They will tend to fall into one of the following categories:

- **Internal:** Feelings, enjoyment, just knowing it within yourself.
- **External:** Feedback, awards, thanks, referrals etc.

Note how much of your feedback falls into either category.

Points of Reference

If your main or only point of reference for knowing you are good at something is the opinions of others – or measures from external sources – you risk discounting your own internal barometer of strengths, feelings and practical skills.

This can lead to poor decision-making.

> **It can be too easy to discount our instinct or self-proven knowledge of our strengths as we look for external validation.**

For example, if you have been told you are no good at writing reports you may shy away from:

- Putting yourself forward for tasks which involve this.
- Furthering your education.
- Applying for a promotion where this skill may be needed.

If, however, you are aware that you are normally good at report writing but didn't do a particularly good job on one occasion – or you are aware it is a skill that needs developing – then you are trusting your own internal barometer.

Thus, you will be more likely to be aware of how you feel when asked to write a report, rather than avoid having to do the task. Self-awareness begins with being honest about:

- What we are good at.
- What we need to develop.
- How we will do that.
- What may stop us developing.

External feedback and references are useful indications for development; however, self-awareness is about learning to accurately assess your own internal barometer.

Without accurate Self-Awareness, you can take on board what other people are saying even if they are wrong.

> **One of the keys to Self-Awareness is starting to question things others say to you – and the things you say to yourself.**

Seeking Opinions

You may still seek the opinion of those you trust and this can provide alternative perspectives.

However, ultimately, learning to trust your internal barometer is an important competency in Emotional Intelligence.

Whilst this may identify areas we wish to develop, it will give us the confidence to start that process. As importantly, it will help us challenge those who disagree or try to generalise our skills, competencies and abilities.

> *A PepsiCo project showed that selecting people based on emotional competencies led to an 87% decrease in executive turnover.*

Here's a way to take this exercise forward. Repeat it for several different areas you have identified you are good at. Write a list of how you know you are good at these areas.

For example, if you are good at an aspect of your job – and say you know this because of "feedback from others" – list this.

In the same way, if you are involved with a charity and you know you are good at something due to feedback, then list "feedback from others" twice – or as many times as necessary.

Continue the process until you build a complete list.

With limited self-awareness we rely on others for all our validation and direction. When we live our lives only by the values and direction of others, we may feel unfulfilled, stressed and discontented.

Communication with Others

If we have limited Self-Awareness, we fail to define our values and thus don't fully know what motivates us.

Our values and motivation determine our intrapersonal communication – the conversation we have with ourselves every moment.

This subsequently determines our interpersonal communication – the discussions we have with others.

How we define ourselves therefore determines our ability to communicate with others.

Therefore if you define yourself only by external achievement the chances are you are only relating to others in the same way.

To build rapport we need to build self-awareness, which in turn builds empathy and this determines how we interact with others.

Using Self-Awareness

Rethinking your Self-Awareness can allow you to make major changes in your life.

Often, this step alone can be enough to allow people to make major steps forward.

However it is also crucial in helping you identify the right competencies to work on in all the areas.

Improved Self-Awareness on its own can often allow you to make major changes in your life.

Case Study: Self-Awareness

Maggie was head of department in a major higher education establishment.

She was recognised as being very good at her job. She had always been very passionate about it and enjoyed the different aspects required.

Nevertheless she reached a point where something did not seem right and she couldn't quite put her finger on it.

When we worked through some of the Self-Awareness exercises, it was notable that she scored low for self-confidence and organisational skills.

I'd known her for a long time and was initially shocked by the results as I felt she'd score very well on both counts. She was equally surprised by the outcome and was beginning to question the process I'd taken her through.

However, I pointed out to her she was answering the questions having recently taken on a new role. Not only had she been doing it a very short time but it was one which, due to a recent restructuring, had never been filled by anyone else.

When we reviewed the results from that perspective, it all made perfect sense. She was working in a situation where there was no existing roadmap or definition of success.

Realising that enabled her to find a way of describing something she'd had a hunch about but had been unable to clarify. Now she was delighted by the process.

Once she had this information and the tools to deal with it, she was totally comfortable about moving forward.

As a result, she saw significant benefits in the power of Emotional Intelligence and the related tools.

4. Improving Self-Management

While Self-Awareness focuses on knowing ourselves, Self-Management is about what we do with that knowledge.

Knowing and doing are two different things.

This is where we start to take responsibility for our own development.

Self-Management is defined as:

> *"Managing one's own internal states, impulses and resources to facilitate rather than interfere with tasks. Being conscientious, recovering well from emotional distress."*

To understand the difference between Self-Awareness and Self-Management, think about the situation where you are shouting at someone.

- If you know you shouldn't be doing it, you have high Self-Awareness.
- If you continue doing it anyway, you have low Self-Management.

Self-Management is about making the decision to do something about it.

As with Self-Awareness, Self-Management is sub-divided into distinct competencies, as follows.

- **Emotional Self-Control:** Ability to avoid reacting to our emotions too quickly.
- **Trustworthiness:** Being someone who is known to be truthful, keeps promises, gives honest opinions and accepts responsibility.
- **Conscientiousness:** Being disciplined and work on a task until it is complete and free of errors or omissions.
- **Adaptability:** Handling change in a constructive manner that benefits others as well as oneself.

- **Optimism:** Remaining focused on something in spite of setbacks or challenges.
- **Achievement Orientation:** Constantly seeking ways to reach goals and meet higher standards.
- **Initiative:** Seeking and seizing opportunities before being required to do so.
- **Commitment:** Remaining loyal and not failing to complete or follow through on a task or promise.

[More detailed descriptions are in the glossary at the back.]

Taking Control

We often find ourselves in situations where we feel we have little control – whether it's at work, within our families or in our personal relationships.

When we are in situations where we feel we have little or no control, we are often focusing solely on the practical tasks.

Thus, in these circumstances, it may be true we have little influence over what is expected of us.

However, we have a lot of control over how we handle ourselves in that situation and how we choose to deal with a given situation at the time.

Even if we feel the need to leave that set of circumstances – maybe change jobs or end a relationship – we can choose how we manage that situation until we have an exit strategy.

> *We have a lot of control over how we handle ourselves in a situation.*

Alternatively, we can find the skills and competencies we need in order to develop ourselves and to influence others so that we can build relationships in those situations.

Again, we can understand this better through an exercise.

Exercise 3: Circle of Trust

Think about a situation where you have an important issue to discuss. Who would you trust to go to? You may have more than one person depending on the situation.

List what it is about that person that makes you want to talk to them.

When we choose to talk to someone about these areas we are looking for particular qualities or competences that build trust and respect for that person.

Your list can be broken down broadly into two separate areas:

- Skills which can be taught.
- Qualities which we can choose to develop.

How many things you listed in the previous exercise are skills and how many are personal qualities?

While we may not have the specific skills required at this moment in time, the personal qualities are totally within our control.

We can choose to be enthusiastic, passionate, helpful or confident. No-one can make us adhere to those qualities. Skills, on the other hand, can be given to us by others.

> *A study of 186 executives showed that those scoring highest on key aspects of emotional intelligence – including empathy and accurate self-awareness – contributed most to profitability.*

Interestingly, our ability to perform those skills well is often supported by the personal qualities we bring to them.

Adopting the right personal qualities can help us more effectively take control of situations – or at least our response to them – so that we are no longer at the mercy of others or events we see as outside our control.

Choosing Behaviour

The emotional competencies in Self-Management allow you to choose your behaviour in a given situation.

When we feel we have control over the situation we are less stressed, more motivated and more fulfilled.

For example, if your Self-Awareness of emotions is high, you determine how relevant they are to that situation and thus you can choose to express yourself in an assertive manner. So you choose whether to develop these Self-Management competencies.

When you make that choice, you influence not only your own development but also the development of those around you.

The more we recognise these Self-Management competencies, the easier it is to improve our Self-Awareness and develop the right competencies.

Let's try another exercise.

Exercise 4: Lifeline

For this exercise, choose a particular time in the past – it may be a day, a week, a month or a particular event that sticks in your memory.

For example it could be a relationship you were in, a job you worked in or just a day that had highs and lows.

You are going to draw a line reflecting how things developed as time went on. It will look a little bit like an ECG graph full of ups and downs.

Turn the following page around and use the start of the line as the beginning of your event – and the end as its conclusion.

Just start the line at any point – wherever the event started and work through it.

When something happened that wasn't great, go down below the line and when it got a little bit better, move the line upwards.

You should identify patterns of thought, feeling and action both when you were feeling low (below the line) and feeling good (above the line).

Take into account what you were thinking, what you were feeling, and what your actions were while this was going on.

You don't want to make this too complicated or in-depth. Just react to your memories and the emotions you felt according to how they were – positive or negative.

The object is to look at what has worked for us in the past and what hasn't.

We're not only raising our Self-Awareness but also identifying when we became aware of situations and started to manage what was happening.

Raising Awareness

The purpose of the exercise is to raise your awareness about how events have influenced your life and how you have managed those events.

This is about how you have started to take control of these situations. The events below the line are valid, genuine and meaningful and at some point in time you have moved away from them.

- Is there a pattern of your thoughts, feelings and behaviours above the line and below the line?
- What were you thinking as you started to move toward the line and then above?
- Can you identify your emotions and the effect they were having on your thoughts and actions?
- Can you identify strategies that you could use in the future to help you cope and manage potential difficult situations or an emotional event?
- When you were above the line, what was happening?
- What where you feeling, thinking and doing?
- Can you do more of this to live a more motivated and fulfilling life? *(Remember, fulfilling may just be enjoying being where you are – we don't always have to be striving for something more, something better. After all, we are Human Beings not Human Doings!)*
- Are the episodes below the line because you have unrealistic self-expectations? *(We often put pressure on ourselves in a way we would never do to others. We talk to ourselves in a critical and unhelpful way; in a way we would never dream of talking to another person.)*
- When you review above the line – can you identify your thoughts, feelings and actions?

Recognising the patterns of your emotions above the line can help you understand your motivations when you are most content and you can apply this to your future goals.

When looking below the line, think about whether it is an external event – something

> *Whatever you are feeling about any issue at any moment is absolutely fine.*

that happened to you. Notice how you dealt with it and remember that you did move on.

You will notice that, in the future, when things are bad again, it's ok to be below the line. You know that you will move on. The more you are aware of this, the more information you have to help you do that when you are ready.

Remember, self -awareness is the key. By identifying how we cope – our internal scripts and subsequent behaviour – we can choose to develop the competencies of Self-Management.

The Power of Self-Management

When people realise there is a separation between Self-Awareness and Self-Management, it breaks everything down into more manageable concepts.

> **When you are aware of something, you can make the decision to do something about it.**

We are often told not to think about how we are feeling and just to "get on with it". However, you now have permission to be aware of how you are feeling.

One of the key aspects of Emotional Intelligence is that whatever you are feeling at any moment about any issue is absolutely fine.

Once you are aware of an issue, you are taking the first step towards doing something about it. You can decide what to do instead of believing that you shouldn't feel that way.

Case Study: Self-Management

Elaine was, by her own admission, an extremely anxious person. She came across as competent as her anxiety drove her to get every task completed, every box ticked. However, she was extremely anxious in her world.

Almost everything seemed to get her feeling she was in a state of high anxiety.

So I asked her to imagine a situation where she got a call to say one of her children had been taken to hospital. There was nothing serious to worry about but they are just being checked over. Not surprisingly, she said she'd feel really anxious. On a scale of 1 to 10, it would be a 12. It'd be off the scale.

Then I asked her to imagine another situation where she had come in from work and put the kettle on. Then, after going upstairs to get changed, she'd come down and realised she'd forgotten to put the lid back on the kettle. The bottom of the cupboards was dripping wet with the steam. She said that would be terrible. She'd be really anxious. It would be a 9 on the scale of 1 to 10.

Then she said: "That's ridiculous."

I didn't have to do anything there. I used the feedback from her, by her using the same language.

I could show her she was seeing everything on this scale and there was very little differentiation in there.

Now that she accepted anxious was ridiculous, I got her to reframe what she was really feeling – to build a better internal dialogue for her.

Often Self-Management is taking a realistic view of a situation and applying the right labels and language so that you can take the appropriate action.

5. Social Awareness

Social Awareness is about how good we are at taking into account the feelings, perspectives and needs of others.

The better we are at this, the more effective we will be at building rapport and developing relationships.

Social Awareness is defined as:

> *"The ability to recognize, perceive and directly feel the emotion of another – often characterized as the ability to "put oneself into another's shoes". Experiencing the outlook or emotions of another being within oneself. Cultivating rapport."*

The competencies are as follows;

- **Empathy:** Ability to recognise, understand and accommodate others' feelings and viewpoints.
- **Organisational Awareness:** Ability to recognise, understand and navigate the structure of an organisation or group.
- **Responsiveness to Others:** Ability to accurately and quickly provide effective advice, assistance, feedback, and recognition to others.

[More detailed descriptions are in the glossary at the back.]

Empathy is one of the competencies but it is also sometimes used to describe the whole category of Social Awareness.

In virtually all areas of our lives – at work or in personal relationships – the way we interact with others is a crucial factor in achieving success.

Working with Others

In anything that involves interaction with another person, you have to be aware of you and of the other person.

The more we are able to put ourselves in someone else's shoes and understand their perspectives, the better we will be at getting the outcome we want. That's where developing skills like building rapport can be very useful.

We often have the tendency to view other people's situations using our own model of the world and our own language. It's extremely useful to develop the ability to see things from the perspective of others.

Building Empathy

One of the key factors to bear in mind when we're talking about empathy and social skills is that there is often a misunderstanding of the language that people use when they are describing or telling you about the emotions they feel.

We typically have quite a narrow vocabulary when it comes to expressing our emotions – if indeed we express them all!

We are usually told "It doesn't matter that you feel like that. Just get on with it anyway."

How many times a day might you say that to yourself? You probably say it to yourself more than to other people.

However, it <u>does</u> matter that you feel like that – because that's what's driving your rational decision making.

> *We often misunderstand the language other people use when they are describing emotions.*

We need to acknowledge that it's fine to be feeling whatever we are feeling and sometimes we need to be able to express that to others.

Maybe we also need to check it out in others so that we can understand how they're feeling.

However, just saying "I understand how you feel" is not quite enough. That's not finding out what they're doing. That's projecting what you're feeling onto them.

Understanding Organisations

Part of social awareness involves understanding certain groups that you are involved with – whether it's social groups or work groups.

You learn "the way we do things around here". There are cultures and sub-cultures. It doesn't mean they will never change but you need to be aware of what they are.

Once you have the awareness, you can choose what to do with it.

Part of social awareness is knowing what else is going on in that environment.

When MetLife selected salespeople on the basis of optimism – one of the Emotional Intelligence competencies – they outsold other MetLife salespeople by 37%.

Developing Integrity

As with any skill, Emotional Intelligence can be used to benefit others or it can be used to manipulate others.

The whole underlying ethic of Emotional Intelligence is based around the intent of the user.

It's valuable to know all of this but it's what we do with it that counts. Using it to develop ourselves and influence others positively is likely to get the best results.

Let's look at some more exercises to get a better idea of how this works.

Exercise 5: Identifying Emotions

Read the following statements and consider each of the described behaviours. Then, for each statement, make a list of the possible words you could use to describe each of the emotions. List all words – without evaluation or dismissal.

1. Clenched jaw, high colour

2. Leaning backward, staring into the distance

3. Narrow eyes and narrow pinched mouth

4. Wide eyed, leaning forward

5. Wag fingers at others - staring directly at them

6. Drop eyes, avoid looking at anyone and droop shoulders.

7. Rolling eyes and fidgeting

8. Fast heartbeat, wide eyed

9. Glaring, may feel hot and flushed

(Adapted from Ciarrochi and Mayer, 2007)

Reading Others

How easy did you find it to identify likely emotions for each statement?

The fact is that some people are more in tune with body language and find it easier to decode than others. However, it's quite likely that you identified more than one option for each of the examples.

It's not always possible to judge what another person is thinking from just one piece of information.

That's why you need to be constantly monitoring the whole communication and taking different elements into account.

Equally, it's important to be aware of what signals you are giving off to others and whether these are constructive or not.

Emotions are contagious. We influence those around us with how we feel and in turn, are influenced by others.

Have you noticed that if someone is happy, if they smile and are optimistic those around are likely to reflect their mood?

Similarly working with those who are predominantly negative can be challenging if you are a natural optimist.

Always take time to check your assumptions about non-verbal communication.

As you have probably seen in this exercise, looking at the same information, we not only may have different opinions to others but can easily have several interpretations ourselves.

Similarly, when we communicate non-verbally we can assume that others have an understanding of how we are feeling and we may think that we are sensing what others are feeling.

Taking time to check your assumptions avoids misinterpretation of other people's feelings or projecting your own feelings or understanding of an emotion onto them.

In Social Awareness, we consider the perceptions of others as well as acknowledging our own.

Expanding our Options

The big challenge for many of us is that expressing emotions does not come naturally to everyone.

We may have been told we need to ignore how we feel, to "get on with the job" or "put on a brave face".

However, unexpressed emotions bubble under the surface and can erupt at any given time.

Our ability to assertively express emotions and recognise them in others is a competence of emotional intelligence.

In order to expand out emotional literacy we often have to develop our language to be able to express our emotions more clearly and accurately.

Taking time to check your assumptions avoids misinterpretation of other people's feelings.

Let's look at what this means through another exercise.

Exercise 6: Increasing Emotional Literacy

Choose an emotion and write it in the centre of the circle below.

Around the outside of the circle place as many alternatives as you can think of which represent your chosen word – if your chosen word was not available.

The words can be stronger or weaker as long as they represent the same emotion.

Finding a New Language

So, how many words did you identify? Are they words you could use if you didn't have your chosen word?

What we can learn from this exercise is that being able to express our emotions in different ways enables us to view them differently and, as a result, get different outcomes.

When we expand our emotional vocabulary, we can be clearer with ourselves about how we feel, thus heightening self-awareness.

This gives us access to a fuller range of emotions which opens up the possibility of reframing any situation we find ourselves in.

We often find that changing the word we use can alter the strength of the emotion and consequently affect the accompanying thoughts and behaviours, dialling them either up or down.

Research in the field of neuroscience by Matt Lieberman has shown the incredible power of dealing with emotional issues. He found that just by saying the emotion we are feeling, we could regain around 10 – 15 IQ points.

> *Changing the word we use can alter the strength of the emotion and affect the accompanying thoughts and behaviour.*

Similarly, following this approach with others, we can check how they may be feeling without telling them just what we see or think.

We can also build rapport more effectively by reflecting the emotions of others verbally and non-verbally.

This is all about expanding our emotional vocabulary so that we can check back with others and also expand our own range of options.

Case Study: Social Awareness

Joe had just taken over as manager of a retail store and became aware that his interactions with Gillian – a key departmental manager – were not going well. He sensed there was an issue between them but was unsure what has caused it.

He responded fairly well to this situation initially by inviting her for a chat and highlighting the fact that things didn't seem to be working well between them.

Gillian welcomed the dialogue and was initially positive about it. However, the conversation became fairly emotional and ended up negatively.

Nevertheless Joe knew that Emotional Intelligence means being able to go back and do something different when things don't work out first time. So he invited her back for another chat which again she responded to positively.

However, having used his Social Awareness to recognise the problem, he did not do such as good job of building empathy.

We often find it difficult to address emotional issues and his initial attempt to get to the root of the issue came across as if he was blaming her. Not surprisingly they again failed to achieve the positive outcome they both wanted.

Rather than give up, Joe tried a different approach and took more time to listen to her views and identify with the issues she was raising. This led to a better dialogue which in turn helped them identify, discuss and resolve the issues.

In this case, some of the elements of Relationship Management we discuss in the next chapter played their part.

6. Better Relationship Management

Relationship Management is about how good we are at using positive influence with others to achieve the best mutually desirable outcome in any situation.

Relationship Management is defined as:

> *"Adeptness at inducing desirable responses in others. Interacting smoothly for co-operation."*

The sub-categories are as follows:

- **Developing Others:** Ability to train others in a supportive manner that fosters personal growth.
- **Inspirational Leadership**: Ability to "rally the troops" to set and meet higher goals by providing a positive example.
- **Influence:** Ability to recognise and manage other people's emotions and to help them to do the same.
- **Communication:** Ability to actively listen to others and speak to them on their own level while offering constructive criticism.
- **Change Catalyst:** Ability to effectively recognise and convince others that change is necessary and to shape the change.
- **Conflict Management:** Ability to recognise conflicts and assist the parties involved to reach a mutually-desirable resolution.
- **Building Bonds:** Nurturing effective relationships with people who could provide assistance now or in the future.
- **Collaboration:** Helping others become more creative and self-sufficient to support individual and collective goals.

[More detailed descriptions are in the glossary at the back.]

Going Beyond Defining the Problem

The range of competencies involved makes Relationship Management the biggest of the four quadrants in Goleman's model of Emotional Intelligence.

As a result, it is a whole topic for study on its own and there is considerable detail on each of the core elements. However, there are three main elements that are the keys to understanding Relationship Management. These are:

- Handling conflict
- Knowing how to communicate effectively
- Encouraging collaboration

When you can get those three elements right, you are well on the way to having effective Relationship Management.

Anyone who has been on a traditional business and corporate training course is likely to be familiar with these concepts already. However, as we highlighted way back in the first chapter, the problem with much of that type of training is that it focuses on "what" the problem is.

- What is conflict?
- What is effective communication?
- What is collaboration?

While this can be useful, we sometimes need to go further than understanding "what" the problem is. We also know "how" we are going to deal with it.

For example, when you form a team to build a raft – and then everybody ends up falling in the water – it's a great way to get to know people. However, this is only really useful if you can then translate that experience back into the workplace.

The key to Emotional Intelligence is that it provides the basis for deciding "how to" make a change rather than simply identifying "what" the situation is.

When You Don't Have Control

Relationship Management, by definition, means that there are at least two people involved and two differing perspectives in any situation. In fact, often there are many different people and perspectives.

We usually don't have direct control over what the others in these situations actually do – even if we have line management responsibility for them. Yet we are often in the situation where we depend on these others to achieve our desired outcome.

> *The emotions of one person in a relationship affect those of the others involved.*

In most situations we therefore rely on our ability to influence in order to get the outcome we want.

The Power of Contagion

As we mentioned in the previous chapter, a key characteristic of emotion is that it is contagious.

We know that the emotions of one person in a relationship affect those of the others involved some way. Negative emotions have a big effect on individuals – lowering their cognitive ability, IQ and to process even the simplest tasks.

That's why it's so crucial to be able to address these issues before they turn into serious long-term problems.

Being able to deal with issues for one person has a positive effect on all the others involved – whether they are people we work with, friends, family, children or parents.

Relationship Management can therefore have a huge impact. We simply need to be able to identify, understand, describe and regulate emotions.

Then we can harness them to improve communication, decision-making and results.

Adapting to Different Perspectives

The big challenge in influencing others is that all people don't behave in the same predictable and consistent way in all circumstances.

Every person brings to any situation their own perspective based on their prior learning, experiences and knowledge. We therefore need to be aware of the emotional perspective and how this affects the way everybody involved thinks and behaves.

In doing this, we can draw together all we have learned about Emotional Intelligence.

Firstly, understanding the perspective of others is crucial so Social Awareness is a key part of that process.

> *Everyone brings their own perspective to any situation based on prior learning, experiences and knowledge.*

However, the one person you have most control over in any interaction is yourself so Self-Awareness and Self-Management are also vital factors in Relationship Management.

When you combine the ability to influence others positively with heightened awareness and ability to manage yourself, you have more chance of getting a better outcome.

We can demonstrate this most effectively by working through another example.

Exercise 7: Perspectives on Emotions

1. Think about an interaction you have been involved in previously that didn't go as you would have liked. It could be a one-off situation or something that happened over an extended period. What was the interaction?

2. What were you doing and saying in that moment?

3. What were you thinking and feeling in that moment? Describe your emotions.

4. What was the short-term outcome of the interaction?

5. What was the long-term outcome of the interaction?

In the next part of this exercise, we go back and look at the same interaction from a different perspective. We can't change the other person who was involved but we can change ourselves. So, we'll consider how we could have approached it differently and how that might have changed the outcome.

6. If this was someone you liked, would you have approached it differently?

7. Where in the process could you have approached it differently – either in your thinking or in what you said or did?

8. How might the outcome have been different if you had done that?

Notice how we can always ask the other person for their feedback at any stage of the process. This may change the direction of the interaction because they may be pleased that we have asked.

Even after the event, we can reflect on what has happened and it is often possible to go back and rerun the interaction with a different perspective.

You can begin to see how the emotional perspectives – your own and those of others – have influenced the outcome.

The question is how you use that information to get better results.

Why People Have Different Perspectives

Many of the factors which determine how we interact with others – our values and our social skills, for example – are formed early in our lives and often depend on our early environment and our parental influences.

Patterns of behaviour and language are typically imprinted when we are children and it can take a great deal of conscious effort to change them.

There are two extremes of parental influence which can be described as "critical" parents and "nurturing" parents.

- Critical parents are always pointing out your mistakes and telling you about your weaknesses.
- Nurturing parents are more positive and encouraging but can be overprotective so not allowing you to develop your own abilities.

Both approaches usually have good intentions in that parents want the best for you. However, the long-term effect of the way they try to do this can sometimes be different from what they intended.

Few parents are at extreme ends of the scale but your confidence, behaviour and communication skills will depend partly on how your upbringing fits into that range.

For example, someone who had more critical parents may doubt their own ability while someone who had more protective parents may have less initiative.

> *People think and behave differently depending on many factors from their past.*

This is not the sort of issue that can be handled on a conventional training course but equally it does not usually have to lead to sessions of psychotherapy.

The key is recognising that people think and behave differently depending on many factors from their past.

Emotional Intelligence provides the framework and language to be able to work around these issues and communicate more persuasively with others. For those who want to go further, Transactional Analysis helps you dip further into how to make changes.

However, by being aware of all the emotional factors, you can find how to communicate most effectively and influence the outcome to the best of your ability.

Relationship Management is about how you collaborate in these situations.

Managing Our Own Contribution

When you are communicating with others – especially if you are involved in a conflict or misunderstanding – one thing you can do is check what you are contributing through your feelings, thoughts, and behaviours and consider the short and long-term outcomes.

It's often too easy to focus on the other person rather than think about what's going on in your own mind.

Dr Phil sums it up well by saying you have to ask if you are contributing to or contaminating a relationship.

In a study of senior executives in an oil company, superior performance was identified by emotionally intelligent behaviours 44% of the time compared to 19% for cognitive intelligence.

When you have strong Self-Awareness, you can think about whether you need to change your own thinking or behaviour in the interests of reaching a better outcome.

Part of using Emotional Intelligence is reflecting on your own contribution to any communication or relationship and considering how that is influencing what is happening.

If we are not honest in the communication we have with ourselves, it is difficult to have a strong and honest relationship with others.

In a sense, one of the key skills of Emotional Intelligence is knowing how to be a good coach – of yourself and of others.

Learning Assertive Communication

Ultimately, one of the keys to influencing others successfully is knowing how to communicate assertively.

> *Communicating assertively is one of the keys to influencing others successfully.*

That is usually something we learn rather than know how to do instinctively. People who have not been taught the concepts usually don't know how to do it. Some adopt it easily while others have more difficulty developing it.

Communicating assertively does not mean being aggressive or trying to dominate others. We need to be aware of how our own communication affects others – what seems like confidence can come over as arrogance, for example.

It is about having the right kind of communication skills to get your point across and achieve a more desirable outcome.

Assertive communication involves learning the right language – both through words and non-verbal communication – to get your message across.

Emotional Intelligence plays an important part in communicating assertively as used in the wrong way, this type of communication can have the opposite effect from what you intend.

Avoiding the Boiling Frog

One of the things that can happen in any group environment is what is known as "boiling frog" syndrome.

Often you have to accept the rules of the environment you are in but, these can change over time and you may find yourself in a situation where you are no longer comfortable and want to get out.

Just as the frog can choose jump out of the steadily-heating pan of water before it boils, you can choose to remove yourself from an environment you don't want to be part of before it's too late.

Not Just For Business

Although much of the language of Emotional Intelligence appears to be suited to a corporate environment, the skills and strategies it teaches can apply in any area of your life.

> *Learning how to communicate with your partner or children is just as important as developing workplace skills.*

In fact, a great deal of the early research into Emotional Intelligence was focused on education and the impact on children.

Relationship Management can just as easily apply to your personal relationships or your role as a parent for example.

Learning how to communicate properly with your partner or children is just as important – often more so – as any skills you can develop for the workplace.

It is a particularly valuable skill to use with children as you can help build their confidence, motivate them to take the right actions – such as doing homework – and give them communication skills that will help in all areas of their lives.

Case Study: Relationship Management

Brian and his three fellow directors were struggling to resolve the challenges that were holding their business back.

They had some divisions that were working successfully but others that were draining their resources.

They needed to make some tough decisions if the business was going to survive at all but they seemed to struggle to reach agreement on the basics. Often it came down to four egos heading in different directions.

The ultimate solution was to address the relationship issues head-on by getting all four in a room together and using many of the traditional management tools to try and work out an agreed strategy.

The challenge is that when these traditional tools are simply focused on the business problems, the result is usually disagreement and failure.

When people are not willing to talk about how they feel and address the emotional issues, they get stuck.

With the right approach to these issues, it was possible to get them all on the same page and to make the key decisions about which parts of the business to close and what strategies to focus on going forward.

In reality, the level of disagreement was not that great. They shared the same objectives and principles. The problem was the agreement was being masked by the degree of personal and emotional noise between them.

When they were able to clear this, they achieved fast agreement and made successful progress.

7. Emotional Intelligence in Action: The Results

Although there has been a growing amount of research and study around Emotional Intelligence is recent years, it is sometimes still seen as being in the category of soft skills that are hard to measure.

Equally some people see the theoretical benefits but aren't sure how they are going to apply it in their business or personal lives.

However, there are many practical examples with specific evidence showing how applying the ideas behind Emotional Intelligence has made a big impact in business and in people's lives.

Many successful businesses have been integrating Emotional Intelligence into their way of working while, outside business, it has been helping individuals change their lives.

This is what The Harvard Business Review said about Emotional Intelligence in 2003:

> *"In hard times, the soft stuff often goes away. But emotional intelligence, it turns out, isn't so soft.*
>
> *If emotional obliviousness jeopardizes your ability to perform, fend off aggressors, or be compassionate in a crisis, no amount of attention to the bottom line will protect your career.*
>
> *Emotional intelligence isn't a luxury you can dispense with in tough times. It's a basic tool that, deployed with finesse, is the key to professional success."*

If those comments were true in 2003, they are likely to be even truer in the light of the changes that have taken place in the world since then.

So it's clear that Emotional Intelligence has not only become part of our everyday vocabulary. Its importance is being increasingly recognised in many areas of our lives.

In this chapter, I share some specific examples of how it has been applied in real situations covering:

- Improving Recruitment and Retention
- Building Leaders and Leadership
- Enhancing Productivity and Building Teams
- Improving Sales and Customer Satisfaction
- Education and Developing Children
- Solving Personal Relationship Issues
- Achieving Overall Life Success and Balance

Improving Recruitment and Retention

Taking on new employees is one of the most expensive aspects of running a business.

You not only have the costs of finding and selecting the right people, you have to train them as well.

However, the hidden cost of recruitment is the cost of replacing people.

- This can arise when you lose well-trained, experienced people who are good at their jobs.
- It can also arise when you recruit the wrong people and they leave quickly – or, even worse, they stay with you and underperform.

It can be difficult for organisations to track this wasted cost as it arises in so many different ways. However many estimates say that around 50% of hiring costs are wasted.

The reality is that companies are often good at testing for skills but few back this up by identifying and assessing the Emotional Intelligence competencies needed to execute those skills.

For example, a candidate for a sales role may demonstrate many of the ideal skills required but if they are not resilient and confident, they will not be a good sales person.

If these competencies are not identified and checked then the recruitment may not be successful.

Retention Benefits

For example, if you assume it costs $30,000 to recruit and train a nurse – though it is often higher – and that the average annual retention is 20%, a hospital employing 200 nurses will spend at least $1.2 million per year on new recruits.

> *A program for developing Emotional Intelligence competencies and reducing stress cut turnover by almost 50%.*

This ignores hidden costs such overtime, employing temporary staff and income which is lost if the hospital is unable to admit patients due to staff shortages.

So, if you can improve retention, you can make significant savings to the bottom line.

That's exactly what happened in one hospital, which had an above-average turnover of 28%. They ran a program for developing Emotional Intelligence competencies and reducing stress. This cut turnover by almost 50%.

That saved them some $800,000 in less than a year.

Recruitment Savings

Another powerful study was done by the US Air Force who wanted to track the financial value of hiring the right people.

They knew that the cost of training Pararescue Jumpers was around $250,000 per trainee and that this was wasted if a candidate failed to complete the training.

In 2009, they conducted a study to identify the effect of Emotional Intelligence on candidates.

They identified five key Emotional Intelligence skills that were highly predictive of who would complete the course.

For example, those candidates who were flexible and adaptive plus optimistic and positive had the best chance of successfully completing the course.

When they applied those competencies in selection, the net savings were some $190 million.

Reasons for Leaving

Another way emotional factors affect retention is that studies suggest that, when people quit their jobs, they are more often leaving their supervisor or manager than leaving the organisation.

The relationship is important but it's the relationship with the person rather than the institution.

Gallup conducts extensive studies on organisational engagement and this has identified three critical factors that predict if an employee is "engaged".

Employees who are engaged are 50% more likely to stay in their jobs.

The employee is most likely to feel engaged when:

- They feel cared for by their supervisor.
- They have received recognition or praise during the past seven days from someone in a leadership position.
- They believe their employer is concerned about their development.

Therefore a leader who has more Emotional Intelligence is most likely to be able to create this kind of engagement.

Building Leaders and Leadership

There is growing evidence of the importance of Emotional Intelligence both as a predictor of leadership skills and as a way of leaders delivering better results.

For example, a study by the British Royal Navy divided participants into two levels of seniority – officers and non-officers.

They were then rated using measures of intellectual, managerial and emotional intelligence competency as well as overall performance and personality.

The study showed that Emotional Intelligence measures were better able to predict overall performance and leadership effectiveness than measures of managerial and IQ competencies.

It also showed that Emotional Intelligence was even more important for senior officers.

> *Emotional Intelligence measures were better able to predict overall performance than measures of managerial and IQ competencies.*

Improving Leadership

As well as helping select leaders, Emotional Intelligence can be a factor in helping leaders lead.

Workplaces that create the right culture and climate tend to deliver higher performance. They lead to higher productivity, better retention and more profit.

Those Gallup studies I mentioned earlier find that almost 75% of the workforce is typically disengaged. Therefore, leaders who are able to foster improved engagement can achieve significant bottom-line results.

Their studies show that teams with higher engagement are:

- 50% more likely to have lower turnover.
- 56% more likely to have higher-than-average customer loyalty.
- 38% more likely to have above-average productivity.
- 27% more likely to report higher profitability.

Clearly leaders with high scores in Emotional Intelligence are more likely to be able to foster better engagement.

Outperforming Others

A project for PepsiCo showed that executives selected based on Emotional Intelligence competencies outperformed their colleagues significantly, achieving:

- 10% increase in productivity.
- 87% decrease in executive turnover ($4m).
- $3.75m added economic value.
- Over 1000% return on investment.

A similar study of leaders in Johnson and Johnson showed a strong link between Emotional Intelligence and top-performing leaders.

Enhancing Productivity and Building Teams

Many studies show the impact of Emotional Intelligence in helping to get the work done.

In one study, top performing sales clerks were shown to be 12 times more productive than those at the bottom and 85% more productive than an average performer.

Only one-third of this difference was identified as being due to technical skill and cognitive ability while two-thirds was said to be due to emotional competence.

Contagion

A key factor in team performance is the role of what is known as "emotional contagion". This is the way feelings spread from one person to another in a team.

> *Positive mood has been found to have a far-reaching effect on work performance.*

The study showed that the mood of the leader influenced group members both individually and collectively.

Research has also identified key emotional factors that have a big impact on productivity.

Four key factors are useful feedback, choice in work, seeing the value of the work, and having a positive climate.

Positive Mood

Positive mood has been found to have a far-reaching effect on work performance, supervision, decision-making, and even on team members voluntarily acting for the good of the organisation.

In a Canadian study, a group of small businesses that had used emotionally intelligent behaviours to help shape the organisational mood or climate saw more revenue as well as increased growth when compared to others.

A study of radiologists found they were more accurate when there was a more positive mood.

In one manufacturing plant, when supervisors received training in emotional competencies, accidents reduced by 50%, formal grievances fell from an average of 15 per year to 3 per year and the plant exceeded productivity goals by $250,000.

Improving Sales and Customer Satisfaction

As Emotional Intelligence is one of the keys to influence, it can make a big impact in the areas of sales and customer satisfaction.

Building relationships is crucial to success in these areas and Emotional Intelligence is an important element in relationships.

There are several studies which show the impact of Emotional Intelligence in this field.

Training

In one pharmaceutical company, salespeople were randomly split into two groups – one of which received Emotional Intelligence training and the other did not.

The first group outsold the second by an average of 12%.

That was an average of $55,200 each, meaning the group of 40 reps who received Emotional Intelligence training sold over $2,200,000 per month more.

The company calculated that they made $6 for every $1 they invested in the training.

Meanwhile sales agents at L'Oreal who were selected on the basis of certain emotional competencies significantly outsold salespeople who were chosen using the company's standard selection procedure.

Those selected on the basis of emotional competencies sold $91,370 more than other salespeople – leading to a net revenue increase of over $2,500,000.

Once again, Emotional Intelligence proved to be a highly reliable predictor of performance.

Performance

Another study of sales performance at Bass Brewers in the UK looked at the relationship between Emotional Intelligence and sales performance.

It found that those with higher self-ratings on Emotional Intelligence had better overall performance – taking into account measures of the number of new accounts sold and employee promotions earned.

American Express found that financial advisors who completed a three-day emotional awareness training increased sales by 2% compared to untrained colleagues.

This was worth millions of dollars in extra revenue as a result of just one three-day program.

Similarly, MetLife salespeople selected on the basis of optimism outsold other MetLife salespeople by 37%.

Customer Feedback

These results also flow through to customer feedback. A study by The Forum Corporation on Manufacturing and Service Companies looked at reasons customers left vendors.

It found that 70% of the reasons related to emotional and relationship factors while only 30% were due to product quality and technical excellence.

Meanwhile, a study of one of the UK's largest restaurant groups, showed that restaurants where the managers had high scores in Emotional Intelligence had better guest satisfaction, lower turnover, and 34% better profit growth than the average.

Education and Developing Children

Many educational experts have believed for some time that young people benefit from a "rounded" education that includes social and emotional development as well as traditional basic skills such as reading and writing.

However, making radical change to the traditional educational approach demands more empirical evidence.

> *Social and emotional learning leads to better results in traditional educational subjects.*

Several studies have suggested that social and emotional learning is not only valuable in itself but actually leads to better results in traditional educational subjects.

One study in New York schools included social and emotional learning programs that, for example, encouraged participating students to write and talk about their own emotions and the emotions they perceived in characters in literature.

The students who participated in these programs had significantly better academic performance, social development and emotional competence than those who did not.

This tends to suggest that a broader educational agenda leads to better results on traditional educational measures as well an in Emotional Intelligence.

Solving Personal Relationship Issues

The issues around relationship problems can seem so personal that it's often difficult to produce hard empirical evidence that appears to apply to every individual.

However one of the most dramatic demonstrations I have seen of Emotional Intelligence in any situation was in the effect it had on one particular personal relationship.

A lady had attended a course I was running on Transactional Analysis and we had been talking specifically about the right we have as individuals within relationships.

The key is that two people in a relationship are allowed to have different opinions. You don't have to accept the other person's point of view on everything.

On the second day of the course, I noticed she looked very uncomfortable and appeared to be holding her head. However, she said she was fine and did not need any help.

The next day, she took me aside and told me the truth. She was in an abusive relationship and her husband had been very unhappy when she went back after the first day and started to stand up for her rights.

He assaulted her and that was the cause of her feeling uncomfortable the next day.

Then, as a result, of the further work we did on the course the second day, she said she kept on hearing the words in her head: "I have a right to be treated fairly."

After having put up with her husband's physical abuse for five years, she called the police for the first time. She was terrified but had never had the strength to do so before.

The knowledge she had gained gave her the confidence to call the police and it changed her life for the better. They even repaired their relationship later.

She really believes the knowledge she gained saved her life. Though I haven't named her here, she has given me permission to share her story as she believes it's important to share the experience in case it helps someone else.

Sometimes Emotional Intelligence and the related knowledge seem like soft skills that are hard to pin down.

However the effect really is that powerful.

In truth, one of the factors that keep me motivated to develop my knowledge and skills in this field is recognising what a huge difference Emotional Intelligence can make in people's lives.

Achieving Overall Life Success and Balance

One of the big attractions of Emotional Intelligence is that it helps you develop and enhance skills that apply to all areas of your life.

While corporate training can make you a better salesperson or a better manager, Emotional Intelligence can help you get more out of your life.

This was proved by a study in the United States of 30 retired National Football League players. It's a fact of life that many professional athletes struggle to be successful in other areas when their career comes to an end. The same applies in fields such as movies and music.

This study found that athletes who scored highly for Emotional Intelligence were much more likely to maintain good health, develop better relationships and avoid problems with drug and alcohol use or violence.

Overall, they were more likely to do well at work and enjoy a higher quality of life than the average.

The Harvard Business review published a survey in early 2012 on the value of happiness. This reflected updating of work I mentioned back in the second chapter which John Kay did in the 1990s.

The conclusion was the wellbeing and emotional resonance of a workplace was one of the most reliable predictors of sustained growth in a business.

So, while it's important to look at the hard financial and other benefits of Emotional Intelligence, its attractions go far beyond the numbers.

Glossary

Emotional Intelligence (EI): The ability, capacity or skill to perceive, assess and manage the emotions of one's self, of others and of groups.

Emotional Competency (EC): A person's competence in developing the ability to express or release emotions.

Emotional Quotient (EQ): A relative measure of a person's healthy or unhealthy development of their innate emotional intelligence.

Emotional Literacy: The ability to recognise, understand, label and appropriately express emotions in ourselves and other people.

Self–Awareness: A realistic assessment of our own abilities; knowing our internal states, preferences, resources and intuitions. Awareness of moods and thoughts about that mood and using those preferences to guide our decision making.

Self-Management: Managing one's own internal states, impulses and resources to facilitate rather than interfere with tasks. Being conscientious, recovering well from emotional distress.

Empathy: The ability to recognise, perceive and directly feel the emotion of another often characterised as the ability to "put oneself into another's shoes". Experiencing the outlook or emotions of another being within oneself. Cultivating rapport.

Relationship Management: Adeptness at inducing desirable responses in others. Interacting smoothly for co-operation.

Glossary of Emotional Intelligence Competencies

The 24 Emotional Intelligence Competencies are defined here and arranged within the four "Clusters:" Self-Awareness, Self-Management, Social Awareness, and Relationship Management -

Self-Awareness Cluster

Emotional Self-Awareness: The ability to read one's own emotions and recognise their impact while using gut feelings to guide decisions.

Accurate Self-Assessment: The ability to correctly measure one's own strengths and weakness; the ability to proportionately assign one's own value and place in a relationship.

Self-Confidence: An appreciation of one's own worth and value; a knowing that one has something to contribute and that one can build on one's strengths.

Self-Management Cluster

Emotional Self-Control: The ability to avoid reacting to one's emotions before those emotions are fully recognised and understood and the most appropriate course of action is decided upon.

Trustworthiness: The character trait that combines honesty, integrity; the trait of being known as one who can be trusted to be truthful, keep one's promises, give honest opinions and accept responsibility.

Conscientiousness: The character trait of being deliberate, disciplined, thorough, able to work on a task or project until it is complete and free of errors or omissions. In terms of Emotional Intelligence, those who are highly conscientious should work to also become highly empathetic and/or more adaptable in order to avoid becoming demanding perfectionists who hold others to impossibly high standards or hinder others' creativity.

Adaptability: The ability to handle change in a constructive manner that benefits others as well as oneself. In the realm of Emotional Intelligence, highly adaptable people who lack assertiveness or self-confidence may be so adaptable that they allow changes to occur that should not and would not if one person in the group were able to suggest or demonstrate a better alternative.

Optimism: The belief that all goals are achievable and that no obstacles are insurmountable; the ability to remain focused on achieving a goal or benefit or resolving a problem in spite of setbacks or challenges.

Achievement Orientation: The mindset that causes one to constantly seek ways to reach goals and set and meet higher goals and standards.

Initiative: The ability to seek out and seize opportunities; the willingness to act early before being required to do so.

Commitment: The character trait of remaining loyal or faithful to and not failing to complete or follow through on a task or promise.

Social Awareness Cluster

Empathy: The ability to recognise, understand and accommodate others' feelings and viewpoints.

Organisational Awareness: The ability to recognise, understand and navigate the horizontal, vertical, and sometimes undefined structure of an organisation or group.

Responsiveness to Others: The ability to accurately and in a timely manner provide effective advice, assistance, feedback, and recognition to others.

Relationship Management Cluster

Developing Others: The ability to effectively teach, assist, support, and train others in a supportive manner and environment that fosters personal growth.

Inspirational Leadership: The ability to "rally the troops" to set and meet higher goals, persevere in times of conflict or uncertainty by speaking and acting in such a way that others desire to imitate the example.

Influence: The ability to recognise, assess, understand and manage other people's emotions and to help them to do the same.

Communication: The ability to actively listen to others' thoughts, ideas, concerns, and opinions and to speak to others on their own level in such a way that their thoughts, ideas, concerns, and opinions are validated; the ability to offer constructive criticism.

Change Catalyst: The ability to effectively recognise, understand and convince others that a change is necessary and to propose the shape, timeframe and extent of the change.

Conflict Management: The ability to recognise and assess conflicts and assist the parties involved to reach a mutually agreeable resolution without assigning blame or fault.

Building Bonds: Creating, building and nurturing effective relationships, with acts of favour and assistance, with people who could provide assistance or become important sources of assistance in the future.

Collaboration: The ability to cooperate with others and to help others become more creative and self-sufficient so that the individual and collective goals of all members of the group are met.

Seven Keys to Success in Emotional Intelligence Coaching or Training

If you are ready to develop your knowledge and experience of Emotional Intelligence, you want to work with someone who can help you move to the next level.

There are several key factors to look out for in a coach or training course that can increase your chance of success.

Here are seven pointers of what you should look out for.

- **Approachability:** Look for someone who is friendly and accessible – who can communicate in terms that are meaningful to you.
- **Knowledgeable:** It should go without saying but look for evidence that they know the subject – both the theory and the practice.
- **Experienced:** Find out how they have applied their knowledge and what results they have seen.
- **Different approaches to learning:** People learn differently so ask about how the training or coaching will work for you.
- **Flexible methods:** Each client or student is different so make sure the training or coaching is tailored to individual needs.
- **Ongoing support:** You need to know you won't be left on your own after the training or coaching sessions. Find out about the ongoing support.
- **Fun:** Finally, Make sure you are going to enjoy it. That's the best way to learn and develop.

Your Next Steps with Emotional Intelligence

I hope this book has inspired you about how Emotional Intelligence can transform your life and that you are ready to explore the possibilities further.

Emotional Intelligence training is a key that can unlock the treasures of self-awareness and success in your personal and professional life.

At Xcellence International, we offer training that can be integrated into your everyday life.

Combining extensive experience in the fields of Emotional Intelligence, coaching and mentoring, we offer a rare blend of solid academic foundation combined with practical application. This helps our clients achieve a holistic command of Emotional Intelligence that ensures they achieve real results.

Xcellence International offers world-class training, which includes:

- Emotional Intelligence Diploma
- Emotional Intelligence Practitioner (see next page for more details)
- Emotional Intelligence Master Practitioner
- Emotional Intelligence Licensed Practitioner
- Coaching Practitioner
- Corporate Coaching
- Personalized Development Programs

Visit our website at the address below for more details, together with further information about Emotional Intelligence and a range of resources including reports, quizzes, DVDs and books on related topics.

Choose the program that will help you reach your full potential and you can soon be among those who attest to the transformational powers of Emotional Intelligence!

If you have any questions or would like to share your experiences of using Emotional Intelligence please email me at colette@ emotionalintelligence-training.com.

www.emotionalintelligence-training.com

Emotional Intelligence Practitioner Training

If you are ready to make Emotional Intelligence work in your life, why not take a look at our Emotional Intelligence Practitioner training?

It starts by giving you a clearer understanding of your own Emotional Intelligence competencies so that you know how to make improvements. You will move from knowing about Emotional Intelligence to living a life informed by its principles.

The program eases the transition from awareness to acknowledgement to action. It is based on a balance between academic theories and practice and this makes it the perfect match for anyone involved in the fields of personal or professional development, management or leadership development.

The practitioner training is an empowering process that allows an individual to get the most out of themselves and the others around them. For example, it is geared toward concrete goals such as:

- Enabling you to grasp quickly what is driving any situation.
- Empowering you to stay in control in moments of crisis.
- Strengthening you emotionally and enabling you to support others.
- Encouraging you to accurately assess personal emotions and show development of emotional vocabulary.
- Creating unique experiences designed to integrate the skills so they can make a difference to your life right away.

The end-goal of Emotional Intelligence training is not just emotional self-awareness but emotional empathy and connection to people around you.

It is about paying attention to what drives human behaviour, being emotionally smart and understanding the true motivations behind your choices.

We would like to thank you for purchasing this book , if you would like more tips on developing your Emotional Intelligence please visit us at

www.emotionalintelligence-training.com